Clydesdale Horses

by Grace Hansen

Abdo
HORSES
Kids

abdopublishing.com

Published by Abdo Kids, a division of ABDO, P.O. Box 398166, Minneapolis, Minnesota 55439.

Printed in the United States of America, North Mankato, Minnesota.

102016

012017

 THIS BOOK CONTAINS RECYCLED MATERIALS

Photo Credits: Alamy, Animals Animals, iStock, Shutterstock

Production Contributors: Teddy Borth, Jennie Forsberg, Grace Hansen

Design Contributors: Dorothy Toth, Laura Mitchell

Publisher's Cataloging in Publication Data

Names: Hansen, Grace, author.

Title: Clydesdale horses / by Grace Hansen.

Description: Minneapolis, Minnesota : Abdo Kids, 2017 | Series: Horses |
    Includes bibliographical references and index.

Identifiers: LCCN 2016944096 | ISBN 9781680809268 (lib. bdg.) |
    ISBN 9781680796360 (ebook) | ISBN 9781680797039 (Read-to-me ebook)

Subjects: LCSH: Clydesdale horses--Juvenile literature.

Classification: DDC 636.1/5--dc23

LC record available at http://lccn.loc.gov/2016944096

Table of Contents

Clydesdale Horses

Clydesdales are big, beautiful horses. Their **unique** look and grand size make them stand out.

Clydesdales were bred in Scotland long ago. They are draft horses. Draft horses are large. They are made to pull heavy loads.

Clydesdales are taller than most horses. They can stand more than 6 feet high. They can weigh up to 2,200 (1,000 kg) pounds!

9

Their bodies are strong.

They have muscular shoulders.

This makes them the best

pulling horses.

11

Clydesdales have strong legs and big feet. One horseshoe can be the size of a dinner plate!

13

These horses have large heads. They have small ears.

Clydesdales come in many colors. Common colors include **bay**, black, and brown.

They have **feathered** white hair on their legs. White markings can appear on their faces and bellies too.

18

Personality & Uses

This big horse is actually very graceful. It walks beautifully. Today, it is a popular carriage and show ring horse.

21

More Facts

- A Clydesdale's feet had to be big to walk on cobblestone roads.

- These horses were **bred** in the 1700s. They come from a place once called Clydesdale, Scotland. Today it is called Lanarkshire, a place that is near the River Clyde.

- Clydesdales can pull many times their own weight.

Glossary

bay – reddish brown.

bred – made to look a certain way and be able to do certain things.

draft horse – a large horse used for pulling heavy loads, especially a cart or plow.

feathered – tufted or fringed.

unique – unlike anything else.

23

Index

abdokids.com

Use this code to log on to abdokids.com and access crafts, games, videos and more!

Abdo Kids Code:
HCK9268